MAUI   JULY 2000

From   KYLE & PAT FIELDS (PILOT)
       1275 PALMETTO PENNINSULA DRIVE
       MT. PLEASANT
       SC 29464

843 - 881 - 7468

KYLE FIELDS 1@ Compuserve.Com

DANGER

DIVING OR JUMPING
OFF THIS TOWER
MAY RESULT IN
SERIOUS INJURIES

G. Brad Lewis

Sunday In™
HAWAII

Library of Congress Catalog Card
Number: 97-73546

First Printing, October 1997
1 2 3 4 5 6 7 8 9

Design by Gonzalez Design, Co.
Layout by Jane Hopkins, Mutual
  Publishing

ISBN 1-56647-174-5

Mutual Publishing
3632 Waialae Avenue
Honolulu, Hawaii 96816
Telephone (808) 732-1709
Fax (808) 734-4094
e-mail: mutual@lava.net

Printed in Hong Kong China

Cat & Kevin Sweeney

D edicated
to all the people within these pages
who took a moment to share their special lives
with us on a Sunday in beautiful Hawai'i.

Mahalo nui loa

Brett Uprichard

Sunday In™
HAWAII
CELEBRATING LIFE IN THE ISLANDS

no PARKING

Ron Dahlquist

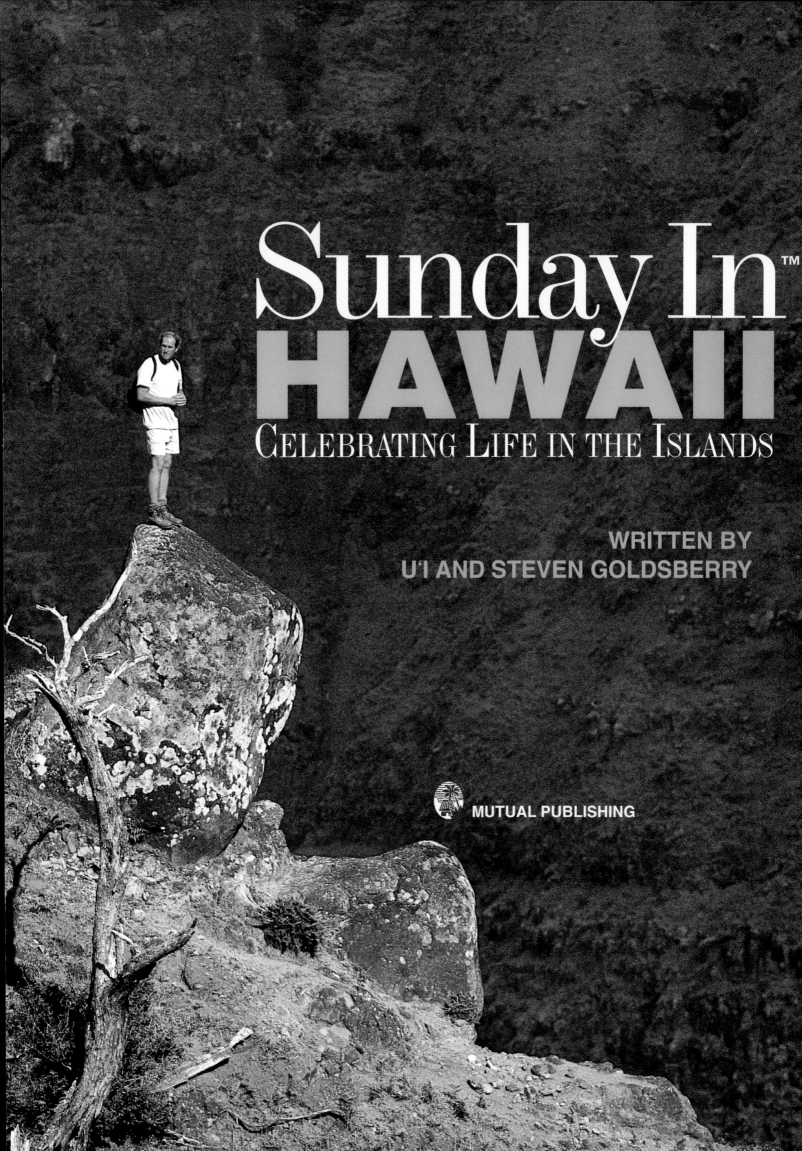

Sunday In™
HAWAII
CELEBRATING LIFE IN THE ISLANDS

WRITTEN BY
U'I AND STEVEN GOLDSBERRY

MUTUAL PUBLISHING

Michael T. Stewart

G. Brad Lewis

Introduction

Sunday! The word alone captures the lustrous spirit of these hours. We have a whole day named for the sun, for basking in life's warm pleasures, for daydreaming or pursuing our brightest dreams, for contemplating the light of wisdom and the fire of wonder. ✿ How we spend our Sundays is who we are. What we like—we do on Sunday. Whom we love—we are with on Sunday. At that someplace we've been meaning to visit—we finally arrive on Sunday. ✿ For some it's a chance to play, or be with neighbors, family, friends, or be alone—a day of fresh focus, a brief vacation. For others it gives us a moment to commune with our gods, whether we go to church or wander the green cathedrals of the rain forest. ✿ Sunday is the time most Islanders revel in their freedoms. Urbanites stream into the country; the highways line with car clubs, cycle cavalcades, and just plain sightseers; stone-calved hikers explore mountain trails and lava fields; weekend yachtsmen decorate the seas with multicolored sails. ✿ In backyards and playing fields the children, our *keiki*, run bases, swing rackets, lose balloons. There are *lu'au* to attend, and barbecues everywhere. There could be a parade; a military base may stage an air show or skydiving exhibition; a school ground could transform with carnival carousels and Ferris wheels. ✿ It's a day to dress up and attend church, a day to dress down and hit the beach. But no matter our attire or where we find ourselves—and whatever the weather—Sunday has a special atmosphere. The hours slow. The demands of deadline and schedule evanesce in the balmy languor of the moment. It's as though liberty is in the air. If on another day of the week someone says, "It feels like a Sunday!" everyone understands. ✿ For many it is the week's holy day, the Sabbath. The word means "to rest." The devout among us honor the Sabbath spirit by taking time to rest, and to reflect on our blessings. In countryside wooden chapels, tucked away beneath palm groves or scented eucalyptus; in urban churches and tabernacles and white-walled temples; on the open rocky pavements of *heiau* terraces—at hallowed places all over the Islands we fashion our most serious rituals of worship. ✿ Less formally, we may visit the cemetery, where we whisper prayers over relatives' graves, or talk to our ethereal ancestors and wait for their response in the leafy murmurings of plumeria trees. ✿ Consciously or not, we come to this day to learn and appreciate, for at last we are free to do so. About this notion the Hawaiians had a proverb: *Ua ao Hawai'i ke 'olino nei malamalama*—Hawai'i is enlightened, for the brightness of day is here. ✿ The photos in this book capture hundreds of moments of such enlightening brightness—all that is worthy and fun and good about the people of our Islands. On these pages you'll see faces and activities that remind you of your own friends and family, and your own Sundays. You'll see things you wish you were doing on Sunday. You'll see your past and future. ✿ How unfair for the rest of the world that we should live not only on the most magnificent islands, but be surrounded by the most beautiful people as well. And that our Sundays are this remarkable.

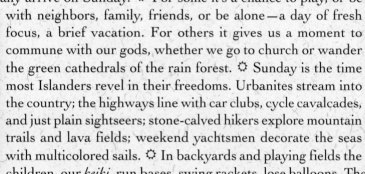

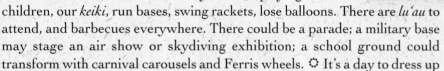

IN THESE GARDENS ARE RECORDED
THE NAMES OF AMERICANS
WHO GAVE THEIR LIVES
IN THE SERVICE OF THEIR COUNTRY
AND WHOSE EARTHLY RESTING PLACE
IS KNOWN ONLY TO GOD
Indicates MEDAL OF HONOR Award

Standing beneath the statue
of Columbia *(left)* — symbol of all grieving mothers — and flanked by the
marble walls inscribed with the names of men and women missing in action in America's
recent wars, a throng of family and friends sings a hymn of remembrance at Punchbowl,
the National Memorial Cemetery of the Pacific. *Franco Salmoiraghi*

· · ·

Bathed in the light of solemn reflection, a visiting clergyman stands
at the nathrex of Saint Andrews Cathedral in downtown Honolulu *(above, top)*,
before Easter mass. *Franco Salmoiraghi*

· · ·

Worshippers hold the hands of *aloha* during Sunday mass at the Holy Ghost Catholic
Church of Kula on the Island of Maui *(above, bottom)*. *Ron Dahlquist*

Ignited by the bright high-altitude rays of early morning *(previous page)*, a colorful crowd witnesses a Sunday awakening of La, the Hawaiian god of the sun, at Maui's Haleakala (House of the Sun). *G. Brad Lewis*

. . .

Like a phoenix rising into green gardens, the Island of Kaua'i has fully recovered from recent hurricanes, its roseate rebirth symbolized by this tranquil Easter Sunday sunrise service at Hanalei *(above)*. *David S. Boynton*

While Sunday is generally a day of rest, for the workers at the Kula Vista Protea farm on Maui it's just another day for loading their buckets of blossoms *(right)*. Protea, Upcountry's treasured exotic flower export, was introduced to Maui in the 1960s by University of Hawai'i botanist David Williams. *Ron Dahlquist*

. . .

Pulling the covers over your head and sleeping in is a great way to start Sunday. *(above, opposite)*. *Franco Salmoiraghi*

. . .

At 6:30 am, a sailor returns to his ship at Aloha Tower after a shore-leave in Honolulu *(below, opposite)*. *Franco Salmoiraghi*

The day every paper boy prepares for *(opposite)*. A budding entrepreneur peddles his heavy Sunday papers on a street in Honolulu. He hopes the headline will lure the Sunday traffic. *Franco Salmoiraghi*

• • •

At the loading dock of the News building, the last batch of Sunday papers waits for delivery in neatly bundled packages *(above)*. By 8:00 am, it's already been a long day. *Twain Newhart*

• • •

This moment of tranquillity began hours before the sun rose *(left)*. The news, printed, packaged, and peddled, is the most reliable element of a Sunday morning reading ritual on the beach. *Twain Newhart*

A little fisherman in his plastic diapers patiently works to untangle his daddy's *hukilau* net. He daydreams, perhaps, of the catch it will bring in, the mesh alive with rainbow-colored wrasses and parrotfish, perfect for Sunday barbecue.
David S. Boynton

Waikiki is the best place to people watch—they watch you, you watch them, and everybody watches out for something unusual *(left)*. Striking theater workers voice their dissatisfaction with contract negotiations at the Sunday opening for *Lost World*. *Chris Mitts*

• • •

For this little parishioner, dressed in a new Easter frock and white patent leather shoes, a colorful Sunday begins with a crayon *(following page)*. Next, maybe a nap, if that sugar-glazed look is any indication. On the steps of St. Andrews Cathedral in downtown Honolulu, the Reverend Dr. Len Howard seems delightfully distracted by this tow-headed *keiki*. *Franco Salmoiraghi*

*A*loha in steel and neon makes for high maintenance *(above)*. A worker, perched on a ladder balanced on a second story landing, cleans the Aloha Tower Marketplace sign on a cloudy Sunday morning. *Franco Salmoiraghi*

• • •

A shopper checks out the merchandise at a Waikiki convenience store before sunrise on a Sunday morning *(right)*. "The worst thing about trying on sunglasses is you have to bend down to look in those little mirrors, and you always have that damn big tag hanging in your eyes." *Susan Aimee Weinik*

Multicolored posters decorate the exterior of this produce stand in Honolulu's Chinatown *(opposite)*. Bananas, oranges, apples, and Chinese cucumber—standard market fare on this side of town—brighten the old sidewalks for the shop's loyal patrons. *Franco Salmoiraghi*

L̲ike horticulturists around the world
(top, left), Hanalei *taro* grower Bill Haraguchi tends to the cultivation of his precious crop seven days
a week. Here, he collects *taro* leaves, the Hawaiian version of spinach.
David S. Boynton

• • •

Weekend hikers on their way to Volcano start their trek in downtown Hilo *(top, right)*. *G. Brad Lewis*

• • •

As eclectic as a Sunday newspaper *(bottom, left)*, this protrait of Hawaiʻi's cross-cultural realities includes
a *lavalava*, a Mexican blanket, and a glass of Florida orange juice. *Franco Salmoiraghi*

• • •

Sunday is the busiest day of the week at Cup A Joe Coffee Shop on the side
of Diamond Head *(bottom, right)*. *Twain Newhart*

On the Island of Kaua'i *(previous page)*, a child feeds the wild chickens under grandpa's watchful gaze in Koke'e State Park.
David S. Boynton

• • •

A young gatherer proudly holds aloft her harvest of Easter eggs *(right)*. Such colorful finds brighten the Easter egg hunt of any child, and any parent will vicariously share in the thrill.
David S. Boynton

• • •

A Tai Chi class meets every Sunday morning at Triangle Park in Kahala *(above, opposite)*. Most of the students are veterans of the art, but join in as much for the camaraderie as for the practice.
Franco Salmoiraghi

• • •

Experienced patrons of Eggs 'N Things on Kalakaua Avenue in Waikiki bring their appetites and Sunday papers to breakfast *(below, opposite)*. The wait is usually 40 minutes, but the food is hearty and delicious and worth the prolonged anticipation.
Susan Aimee Weinik

Hawai'i's history
and culturally rich heritage abides in the faces
of its people. The blending of native Hawaiians with
races from around the world is visible in our children's
eyes, our grandparent's chins, the texture
of our hair.   Over half of the marriages performed in
the Islands are interracial. Such mixing
has increased through the generations. Ask a
citizen of Hawai'i his or her racial extraction and
the answer often runs something like: "I'm
Hawaiian-Chinese-Filipino-Portuguese-Swedish-
Apache."   The traditions we celebrate, songs
we sing, and our leisure activities are reflections of
these ethnic mixes. Hawai'i's children ride horses and
learn the skills of the paniolo, we dance the dances of
Polynesian Islands far to the south, and we adorn
ourselves with flowers brought here from Africa,
Europe, South America, and Asia.   We take pride
not only in our tolerance of each other's dissipating
differences, but in our embracing of those differences.
This is the truest expression of aloha, that precious
philosophy the ancestral Hawaiians taught
by universal and daily example to the
malihini, the newcomers.

(from top, left to right:
Susan Aimee Weinik, G. Brad
Lewis, Ray Mains, Franco
Salmoiraghi, Cat &
Kevin Sweeney)

(from top, left to right: David S. Boynton, Franco Salmoiraghi, Richard A. Cooke, III., G. Brad Lewis, G. Brad Lewis, Ray Mains, Ray Mains)

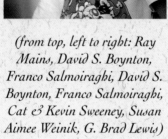

(from top, left to right: Ray Mains, David S. Boynton, Franco Salmoiraghi, David S. Boynton, Franco Salmoiraghi, Cat & Kevin Sweeney, Susan Aimee Weinik, G. Brad Lewis)

(from top, left to right: Chris Mitts, Cat & Kevin Sweeney, G. Brad Lewis, David S. Boynton, G. Brad Lewis, Ray Mains, Cat & Kevin Sweeney, G. Brad Lewis)

Each
Sunday morning,
over a hundred elderly
Filipino men and women
gather on the corner of
Fort Street and Hotel in
downtown Honolulu for
coffee and casual
reminiscence *(opposite)*.
Franco Salmoiraghi

✦ ✦ ✦

A little cyclist escorts
her mom and dad on their
Sunday jog through a park
on the Big Island *(above)*.
G. Brad Lewis

Boogie boarders,
holding their emblems
of athletic ability high
above their heads *(left)*,
make their way down
Waikiki's Kalakaua
Avenue to the beach.
Twain Newhart

Rock climbing, a craze on the mainland *(opposite)*, has taken a toehold here in the Islands. Enthusiasts take to Hawai'i's volcanic mountains, testing their strength and skill against this geologically young terrain. *Twain Newhart*

* * *

Some climb mountains while others prefer peaceful reverie *(left)*. On Kaupoa Beach on the Island of Moloka'i, lounging in a soft pink hammock under a regal blue sky is a wonderful way to spend a Sunday afternoon. *Bronwyn Cooke*

* * *

Participants in the Great Trans-Ko'olau Race wait at the starting line *(following page)*. *Franco Salmoiraghi*

These mini beach bunnies insisted they could
take better shots than our pro *(top, left)*. While they confused themselves with the viewfinder of a decoy camera,
David Boynton, the *Sunday in Hawaiʻi* photographer for Kauaʻi, snapped a quick one. *David S. Boynton*

* * *

The art of bamboo cultivation is as much a meditation as a harvest *(top, right)*. *Franco Salmoiraghi*

* * *

Sunday brings in the most tourists for this Polynesian woodcarver and his hand-hewn *tiki (bottom, left)*. *Chris Mitts*

* * *

Wearing swim suits and casual shirts, the ministers of Hope Chapel baptize a new member
in the waters off Kihei on the Island of Maui *(bottom, right)*. *Ray Mains*

Bait fishing in Honokohau
Harbor has been real good lately. Who needs a boat when
all of your friends, with their hats of identical straw plait
and their coolers filled with icy beer, can meet on the
dock and make a day of it? *Cat & Kevin Sweeney*

A group of local kids and a dog send out a big *aloh*a from Kailua-Kona on the Big Island *(left)*. *Kirk Lee Aeder*

• • •

This Sunday gardener takes a few minutes from harvesting her salad greens for some friendly advice from the *obasan* next door *(above)*. *Franco Salmoiraghi*

A crowd of *paniolo*
(above) watch a calf roping event at the Haʻahea
Cancer Benefit Rodeo at the Maliko Bay Rodeo Arena on
Maui's north shore. *Ron Dahlquist*

• • •

You can almost read the hymn lyrics
over the shoulders of these Kalaupapa parishoners
(right) as they celebrate Sunday mass in Father Damien's
church, St. Philomena, on Molokaʻi. *Richard A. Cooke, III.*

• • •

Children straddle a parking lot fence
at the rodeo *(above, opposite)*. This spot has two
advantages: you get a better view and you can pretend
you're riding a horse. *David S. Boynton*

• • •

A determined *paniolo* roping team works hard
to bring down a running steer *(below, opposite)*.
Ron Dahlquist

Where
there's smoke there's
sure to be fire *(opposite)*,
and where there's savory
teriyaki shishkabobs there
are sure to be smiles.
Franco Salmoiraghi

• • •

There are those who create
life's dramas and those who
sit on the side and watch
(above). On a stone wall
above a pond in Honolulu's
Ala Moana Beach Park, a
little girl listens to the
animated chatter of her
three friends.
Chris Mitts

• • •

On Hotel Street in
Chinatown, shoppers
wait for "Fasi's Limousine"
(the Bus) after a Sunday
morning at the markets
(left). Franco Salmoiraghi

37

Warmed by the heat of naked bulbs, Char Siu-coated roast duck and ribs hang in the Chinese market in Chinatown, Honolulu *(previous page)*. The interior of the market is red. Chinese restauranteurs believe that the color makes customers feel hungry.
Franco Salmoiraghi

⋯

Benny Orso, a Big Island entrepreneur, packs a shave ice cone tight with a rubber-gloved hand *(right)*. *Cat & Kevin Sweeney*

⋯

Patrons in a plush paradise look for bargains at Pearl City's Kamehameha Drive-in swap meet *(above, opposite)*. Once a favorite Saturday night movie venue, today this outdoor landmark is O'ahu's largest used merchandise Sunday shopping value.
Julie Sotomura

⋯

A calabash auntie shares a *luau* cup of *kalua* pig with her hungry *keiki* at the Sunday Seafest in Kihei on Maui *(below, opposite)*. *Ray Mains*

Bent double with
exhaustion, a team of lifeguards gasps for breath at the
Waikiki finish line for the Hawaiian Oceanfest *(opposite)*,
an annual water sports and open ocean rescue
competition. *Twain Newhart*

Athletes join sunscreen
spectators for cold brew and some shaded
breeze between games during a volleyball tournament at
Kuhio Beach *(above)*. *Twain Newhart*

43

We jump into water—from bridges and rocks, from piers and pylons, from sea walls and waterfalls. We jump for the cooling. We jump for the fun. We jump for the liberation of the fall. Is there any other way, for a few brief moments, to feel the flight of a bird, the weight of a rock, and the buoyancy of a fish? ⬦ Take a deep breath, plug your nose, and release yourself to the air. It's the sweetest expression of spontaneity. An unabashed free fall with boards tucked under arms ends in a raucous splash between waves, and begins a surfing session. No matter what your age, if it's a Sunday and you're near deep water with a tower of stone or steel above it, take the leap. The memories of those "hana budda" years will rush up to meet you.

(opposite page—from top, left to right: Ray Mains, G. Brad Lewis, G. Brad Lewis, Ray Mains, G. Brad Lewis, Twain Newhart [bottom series]; this page—from top, left to right: Ray Mains, Lauren Lavonne Pritchett, Julie Sotomura; following page: photos by Julie Sotomura)

At Twelve Palms Beach in Waikiki,
the smoke of Sunday hibachis announces the happy arrival of sizzling teriyaki chicken,
a gastronomic tradition for Hawai'i get-togethers *(top, left)*. *Susan Aimee Weinik*

Percussion musicians gather to pound out the rhythms of their heritage
in a Sunday drumming circle at Kualoa Beach Park *(top, right)*. *Franco Salmoiraghi*

Each Sunday afternoon the Cigar Room in Kaimuki opens its doors for patrons to share
a moment of lighting up and leisure *(bottom, left)*. *Julie Sotomura*

The aristocratic taste of polo season—mimosas and strawberries, barbecues and beer—
attracts spectators to the Sunday matches at the Mokule'ia field *(bottom, right)*. *Franco Salmoiraghi*

Mini regattas dominate the ponds in Ala Moana Beach Park on Sunday afternoons *(above)*. Craftsmen test and sail their radio-controlled boats just a few feet from the Honolulu Yacht Club.
Twain Newhart

• • •

"FREE AT LAST" says it all *(right)*.
Gary Hofheimer

• • •

Near the Natatorium in Waikiki, a lone guitarist ponders the emotions evoked by his music *(opposite)*. Sunday strumming can make a man feel like a king, even if his throne is a picnic table in a public park.
Lauren Lavonne Pritchett

Young baseball fans keep up their patient wait for their heroes to complete the senior walk around the bases at Rainbow Stadium. On this Mother's Day Sunday these future collegians watched the University of Hawai'i "Base Bows" win the last game of the season, against San Diego State. It may be impossible for all of these loyal admirers to follow in the cleated footsteps of their favorite Rainbow, but many, now active in Little League teams around Honolulu, will return to their home diamonds and practice their pitching, batting, and catching skills in diligent pursuit of the dream. What better gift for a mom on Mother's Day than to have her little one aspire to become a college athlete.
Franco Salmoiraghi

• • •

Standing in full uniform on the docks of Kewalo Basin, the King's Guard from King's Village in Waikiki are presented for review *(following page)*.
Gary Hofheimer

It's a wise merchant
who creates a space for men to congregate and talk while
the women busy themselves with hunting for bargains
(above, opposite). Franco Salmoiraghi

• • •

This young hostess
gingerly serves up fruit punch
and cupcakes to friends who came to call
for a Sunday morning tea *(below, opposite)*. G. Brad Lewis

Weary shoppers and hungry birds
throng the upper deck of Center Court at Ala Moana
Shopping Center *(above)*. Twain Newhart

On Sunday morning *(left)* —
and every other day of the week — the Fresh Market in
Manoa serves up breakfast, lunch, produce, and a mellow
venue for friendly conversation. Ian Gillespie

Members of the Bike Way cycling team
peer ahead to see who's leading the pack in a race
through the back streets of Waimanalo *(following page)*.
Lauren Lavonne Pritchett

"E nei,
braddah! Get one ladda!"
G. Brad Lewis

Beach volleyball games on the broad, white sand fronting Fort DeRussy and the military's Hale Koa Hotel in Waikiki is the perfect place to guy watch and take in some glowing sunshine.
Lauren Lavonne Pritchett

An engraver spends
his Sunday *(above, opposite)* crouching low among
the black and grey monoliths of a cemetery in Hilo on
the Big Island to etch a name on a tombstone.
G. Brad Lewis

• • •

Every Sunday *(below, opposite)*,
the First Federal Savings Fort Street Mall and
Merchant Street office gets a clean view
of the world. *Chris Mitts*

• • •

"Ho, man, you wen see me! I was cookin'.
Nex time, I goin' bus da spin moves!" *(above)*
Cat & Kevin Sweeney

• • •

"Only fifty cents. Yeah, it's a vase,
but you can use it for beer, or to put those
extra pennies in, or whatevas. It's a bargain." *(left)*
In Manoa, families, friends, and entire neighborhoods
gather to recycle their household items and unwanted
Christmas gifts at garage and yard sales.
Franco Salmoiraghi

The deep blue of the
waters off Honolulu and Waikiki churn as Hawai'i's
yachting community takes to the seas in blasts of
spinnaker color *(left). Twain Newhart*

. . .

Like a scene from a Hollywood movie *(above)*,
this mother and child rest on the dark sands of the
Big Island next to the rustic rigging of an
outrigger canoe. *G. Brad Lewis*

The beautiful red fighting roosters, originally brought in from South America and the Philippines, are now family pets *(right)*. It's rumored that Sunday cockfighting continues in many rural areas on all Islands.
Twain Newhart

∙ ∙ ∙

Three butts to the wind *(above, opposite)*. The *Mauna Lani Flash*, a racing yacht, prepares to take on the winds and waves off Waikiki.
Gary Hofheimer

∙ ∙ ∙

A good night of "squidding" yields a string of dangling tentacles on the shore at Kualoa Beach Park *(below, opposite)*. The reefs near Chinaman's Hat in Kane'ohe Bay are ideal for this kind of harvest.
Twain Newhart

On the Sunday of Memorial Day weekend, Vietnam vets mounted their "hogs" and rode in cavalcade through downtown Honolulu and up the winding road to Punchbowl, the National Memorial Cemetery of the Pacific. They parked their choppers—chrome polished to a high sheen, leather waxed, and tires buffed—in military precision along the boulevard leading to the "Courts of the Missing," and took their places among the crowd of loved ones and friends. The program featured a military color guard, band, helicopter fly-over, candle-light vigil, and much prayer in commemoration of the service men and women whose bodies were laid to rest in the hallowed ground of this ancient volcano crater.

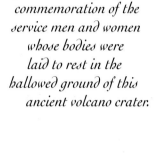

(opposite page—from top, left to right: Franco Salmoiraghi, Twain Newhart, Franco Salmoiraghi, Franco Salmoiraghi, Twain Newhart; this page—all photos by Franco Salmoiraghi, cutout photo by Chris Mitts)

Lined up to receive
last minute instructions, these gallant knights and their well-trained
steeds prepare to wage a sham battle on the polo field *(top, left)*. *Franco Salmoiraghi*

* * *

Spectators savor a Sunday of brunch, lunch, barbecue, and beer as they watch
the ancient sport of kings *(top, right)*. *Franco Salmoiraghi*

* * *

At full gallop, Peter Baldwin *(bottom)*, a decendant
of the families that founded the Alexander & Baldwin company
in the late 1800s, upholds a family tradition by playing polo
on Sunday afternoon in Upcountry Maui. *Ron Dahlquist*

The horse seems to be saying "Oooooo!" as he bucks this hapless polo player from his back, at the first Sunday practice for the Anini Beach Polo Club on Kaua'i. *David S. Boynton*

An outrigger canoe team talks strategy
before paddling in the 8th Annual Business Canoe Race on Kaua'i's Wailua River *(top, left)*. *David S. Boynton*

• • •

Local beauties wait in their black-framed bed "float" for the start of the
24th Honolulu International Bed Race parade in Kapi'olani Park *(top, right)*. *Franco Salmoiraghi*

• • •

Local girls in Maori outfits *(bottom, left)*, part of a Polynesian dance group,
excitedly await their turn on the field for the Pro Bowl halftime show at Aloha Stadium. *Lauren Lavonne Pritchett*

• • •

Covering the event for ESPN, KHNL newsman Dan Cooke interviews
rough-terrain cyclists at the International Mountain Bike Competition at Kualoa Ranch
(bottom, right). *Franco Salmoiraghi*

Loading up a vintage 1974 "Thing" with boards, kids, coolers, and parents, the Steve Macres family gets ready for a Sunday surfing safari on Maui.
Ron Dahlquist

A stretch, a lift, and an elongated frame begins a classic ballet chassé at the Honolulu Dance Company studio in Honolulu's Waterfront Tower *(above)*.
Franco Salmoiraghi

• • •

Ballet stretches the laws of physics *(right)*. Taut muscles lift the center of gravity to mid-torso and free the dancer for light, fluid movement.
Franco Salmoiraghi

A pair of glass doors separates the brute force of the weight room from the graceful elegance on the dance floor *(left)*.
Franco Salmoiraghi

• • •

Over time, the discipline of dance will transform the hesitant and wobbly balance of these youngsters into the coordinated élan of the stage *(above, top)*.
Franco Salmoiraghi

• • •

A jazz dance teacher molds her protégé's body into an arabesque *(above, bottom)*. Muscles are held in tension long enough for the cells to memorize the position. In this way, the classic postures will become a natural part of the body's expression. *Franco Salmoiraghi*

The artisians take a break outside their
woodworking shop, Kamani Woodworks, in Kakaako for some liquid refreshment *(top, left)*. *Ian Gillespie*

• • •

Mel Cachola, a master short-order breakfast chef, takes a breather during the Sunday morning rush
at Honolulu's Liliha Bakery Coffee Shop. *(top, right)*. *Franco Salmoiraghi*

• • •

In an apothecary's treasure house *(bottom, left)*, the Pill Box drugstore
in Kaimuki, Dr. Mac spends his Sunday filling prescriptions. *Franco Salmoiraghi*

• • •

A cookie break in the shade of the Leonard Jr.'s Hot Malasadas wagon always makes life
a little sweeter *(bottom, right)*. *Ian Gillespie*

Security guards at the Contemporary
Museum say their Sunday patrons are as colorful as the artwork *(top, left)*. *Franco Salmoiraghi*

• • •

A pair of sunglasses, a cup of latte, and the Sunday *New York Times*
are the best way to recover from a Saturday night on the town *(top, right)*. *Franco Salmoiraghi*

• • •

When these kids' parents *(bottom, left)*, exhausted from a morning of bed racing,
relinquished control of their stripped-down craft, it became a fire engine, then a chariot, and then an intergalactic
battle cruiser manned by Commander Reebok and his space warriors. *Franco Salmoiraghi*

• • •

Watched over only by Marilyn and Mao *(bottom, right)*, a worker finds
peace and inspiration in his solitary Sunday hours at the office. *Franco Salmoiraghi*

A chain-link frame on unchained spirits: Senior Softball League games are played at Maui's War Memorial Field every Sunday during spring and summer *(above, opposite)*.
Ron Dahlquist

A balloon-toting *keiki* admires the view as neighborhood families gather for Sunday morning warm-ups in Kapi'olani Park *(below, opposite)*. Tai Chi classes are offered here as well, with majestic Diamond Head looming in the background.
Franco Salmoiraghi

After enduring the chaos of their weekly jobs *(above)*, members of Mililani's 24-Hour Fitness regain their focus in the pool's ordered lanes and predictable distance of bright water… *Ian Gillespie*

…while the more serious-minded *(left)*, on this Sunday morning, bend to weightier tasks in the Club's new workout room. *Ian Gillespie*

Harry, James J. J. Keola, and
Jonah Pono Hueu *(above, opposite)*, *taro* farmers on Maui's famed Keʻanae
Peninsula near Hana, stand just slightly taller than their healthy
green crop of Hawaiʻi's native staple. *Ray Mains*

. . .

A young Maui fisherman looks for the perfect spot
to set up his fishing station for a Sunday of working
the waters *(below, opposite)*. *Ray Mains*

. . .

Hopeful *oʻopu* fishermen *(above)*, settled in along the banks
of Kauaʻi's Hanalei River, work their lines through the
chocolate-colored water. *David S. Boynton*

Liokai

L*iokai* translates to sea
horse. These *keiki* are having a tough time getting
into the saddle *(previous page)*. *G. Brad Lewis*

• • •

Following an Easter sunrise service,
a young family enjoys breakfast on a bench outside
the Waiʻoli Mission Hall in Hanalei, Kauaʻi *(above)*. With
plate in one hand and fork in the other, Dad coaxes his
son into a bit of rice. But Jr. is more interested in
what his older sister is eating. *David S. Boynton*

A popular form of football in Europe and the Islands of the South Pacific, the sport of rugby has attracted a grassroots following in Hawai'i *(above)*. Local teams have soared to the challenge, and even play host to international tournaments here. *Brett Uprichard*

• • •

"Hey, Mom? *(left)* What's that long, green squirty thing? Is it a vegetable? Looks like one. We're not taking it home are we? Are you going to make me eat it? Mom?"
G. Brad Lewis

"I'm in. Can I catch a ride to the waves?" *(above)*
Twain Newhart

• • •

Hanging canoe paddles create an impromptu chandelier of sunlight and wood *(right)*.
Twain Newhart

• • •

The crowd yells as canoe teams pull toward the finish *(above, opposite)*.
Twain Newhart

• • •

Outrigger canoe clubs from all the Islands compete in the regatta season *(below left, opposite)*. The racers are divided into two groups— short-distance sprinters and long-distance open ocean teams.
Twain Newhart

• • •

Aloha means hello *(below right, opposite)*. An interisland flight approaches landing as the last canoes cross the finish line at Honolulu's Ke'ehi Lagoon.
Twain Newhart

A local fisherman
bathes his one-year-old son in a warm tide pool at
Moʻomomi Beach on the Island of Molokaʻi *(opposite)*.
The child was born three months ago at the hour, at this
place, in this pool, near the spot where his parents set his
"*piko*." *Margo Berdeshevsky*

* * *

Two of Hawaiʻi's sons *hoʻokani pila*,
play music *(above)*. They sing a *kolohe* song about
rascally things that cannot be detailed here.
Margo Berdeshevsky

Artist Jan Kasprzycki's
pallet takes up an entire table in his studio in Olinda,
Maui. The vibrant colors are the trademark of his lush
tropical oils. *Ron Dahlquist*

· · ·

You'd think the animals in the mural
were alive judging from the excitement displayed
by these patrons of the Honolulu Academy of Arts
(above). *Franco Salmoiraghi*

· · ·

A statue of Penelope *(left)*, sculpted by
French artist Antoine Emile Bourdelle, presides over the
Sunday stream of visitors to the central courtyard at the
Honolulu Academy of Arts. *Franco Salmoiraghi*

· · ·

Encirled by *lei* and well-wishers,
Auntie Caroline De Lima celebrates
her 80th birthday after the service at
Keawali Congregational Church
on the Island of Maui *(following page)*.
Ron Dahlquist

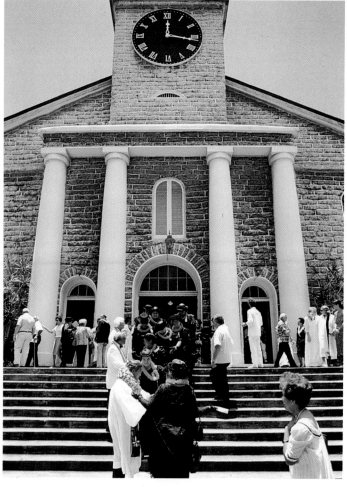

Singing hallelujahs
to the sky *(opposite)*, Kihei's Hope Chapel chorus
offers a dramatic performance to the congregation
on Easter Sunday. *Ray Mains*

Adorned in formal
black *holoku* and golden *'ilima lei*,
members of the Ka'ahumanu Society descend
the stairs of Kawaiaha'o Church in a cascade of dignity
(above). Reverend Kaina greets the noble procession.
Each *"Ali'i* Sunday" the Daughters of Hawai'i,
the Ka'ahumanu society and other benevolent
organizations gather for special services
to celebrate the birthdays of Hawai'i
royalty. *Lauren Lavonne Pritchett*

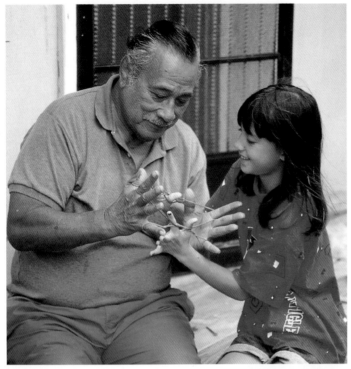

Kupuna and *keiki* share a
moment on the back porch with fingers wrapped with colored strings *(top, left)*.
Who is teaching whom to play the age-old game of cat's cradle? *Sri Maiava Rusden*

It's Sunday, it's hot, and the papers weigh a ton *(top, right)*.
This casual and cool paperboy lets a very good product sell itself. *Sri Maiava Rusden*

No one looks like they're having fun *(bottom, left)*. The smiles come out
when the soap is gone, and the towels are thrown in the wash. *Sri Maiava Rusden*

Fishermen take their catch to the streets,
with hand-painted signs, ice chests, and bargain prices *(bottom, right)*. *Sri Maiava Rusden*

(this page—from top, left to right: Cat & Kevin Sweeney, Bronwyn Cooke, Ray Mains, G. Brad Lewis, Julie Sotomura)

Like the garden of Eden, Hawai'i's paradise is filled with extraordinary animals. We share our lives with our pets. They might be small enough to carry on a finger—a green chameleon to accentuate a red swimming suit. They might make us laugh, or laugh at us, like that mule on Moloka'i who finds humor in what the tourist lady stepped in. We take them for walks, and they take us. They dance, they sing, they smile for the camera. They're so nearly human, we love them like we love our own kids, even if we're just kids ourselves. They ride with us: in the family car, or on our heads. We might put a helmet and goggles on them and whisk them about in the sidecar of a red motocycle. We dress them up and cool them off, and feed them whenever they ask. We love our pets — our fine feathered, scaly, and furry friends — and they love how we love them.

(this page—from top, left to right: G. Brad Lewis, Franco Salmoiraghi, Twain Newhart, Twain Newhart, G. Brad Lewis, Twain Newhart, Ray Mains)

97

Trying to outrun the snarling maw of a North Shore monster *(previous page)*, this Waimea Bay lifeguard guns the throttle and bolts to the safety of the inner reef.
Gary Hofheimer

• • •

Sunday surfer Buzzy Myer races his pilot, Sierra Emory, across a bright face of deep-water blue *(right)*. Tow-in surfing originated on the Island of Maui at a surfbreak called Jaws. Professional watermen Jerry Lopez and Laird Hamilton pioneered this dangerous sport where surfers are towed by jetski into huge outside cloudbreaks—a good way to avoid Sunday crowds. Special big wave "guns," modified with foot straps, allow the surfer to ride out like waterskiing slalom. The jetski then pulls him into the rising swell, he drops the tow-line, and rockets down a wave 20- to 60-feet high.
Ron Dahlquist

"You see that one? *(top, left)*
He's riding the wave. Oh! He's falling! Oh! See his feet? This place is called Sandy Beach?
Is that because the swimmrs all roll around in the sand? *Lauren Lavonne Pritchett*

. . .

"I can do this. *(top, right)* See, all those little kids are doing it.
They don't even have boards. I've got a board. I can do this." *Lauren Lavonne Pritchett*

. . .

"Shaka, braddah! Howzit, boo!
No ways. No can surf wit dis ca. No room fo da board." *(bottom, left) Lauren Lavonne Pritchett*

. . .

"Harry up! Go fasta! Get one swell at Sandy's! We goin' miss 'em."
(bottom, right) Lauren Lavonne Pritchett

A windsurfer skips over
the churning inside whitewater to distance himself from
the raw thunder of the waves *(above)*. *Gary Hofheimer*

· · ·

These aren't the wings of a sea angel *(above, opposite)*,
they're just beach mats spread against the freshness of a trade
wind to clean sand from the weave. *Franco Salmoiraghi*

· · ·

It's a beautiful day for swimming al fresco
and feeling as free as the sea at Mahai'ula *(below left, opposite)*.
Cat & Kevin Sweeney

· · ·

These soft little waves in Hanalei Bay on Kaua'i
might be too easy to ride standing up *(below right, opposite)*.
Besides, this is a good way to see what's
following you. *David S. Boynton*

Duke Kahanamoku's
outstretched arms of greeting become an embrace
for this young man as he reads about the legacy of
Hawai'i's Olympic swimmer, champion surfer, and
Ambassador of *Aloha (above, opposite).*
Franco Salmoiraghi

. . .

Surfers play chess while waiting
for the promised swell *(below, opposite).*
The waves don't keep their appointments
on Sunday either. *Twain Newhart*

. . .

"GO!" Pro watermen splash into competition
at the annual Hawaiian Oceanfest *(above).*
Twain Newhart

$\mathcal{S}$urfers, like their trusty boards,
come in all shapes and shades *(opposite)*. Future champion Cody Welsh poses at dawn
on his way to a morning of floaters and cranking bottom turns. *G. Brad Lewis*

· · ·

A troop of rough-water swimmers *(above)*,
their entry numbers displayed all over, waits at the starting line of a *keiki* meet. *Gary Hofheimer*

· · ·

At the Chinese cemetery in Manoa Valley,
the spring rituals of the Ching Ming ceremony include the burning of paper money *(following page)*.
Its essence rises with the smoke into the heavens so the dead ancestors will have
money to spend. *Franco Salmoiraghi*

A young juggler stands in the blurry swirl of multi-colored batons in Wailoa State Park on the Big Island *(right)*.
G. Brad Lewis

• • •

Kumu hula Namahana Kalama-Panui beats the ancient rhythms of the chant for her *Na Mamoali'i O Kauiki* dancers at an *Au I Ha Kai 'Ewalu Makeke* performance *(below)*.
Ray Mains

• • •

Oils and acrylic artist Edie Hansamut *(opposite)*, with a makeshift rock easel, lets the motion and sound of these tiny waterfalls inspire her as she paints the Honoulimalo'o Valley stream on the Island of Moloka'i.
Richard A. Cooke, III.

W atched over by fanciful
statues in his garden, Catalino "Pete" Agliam of Lana'i
mends his fishing net while the plumeria tree drops
blossoms at his feet *(previous page)*.
Ron Dahlquist

• • •

The serenity of the Anahola River
provides a Sunday venue for a sibling dance called
"rock 'n' roll rowboat." *(above) David S. Boynton*

The Sandy Beach Local Chef serves up hot
and cold Hawaiian flavors to surfers, beachcombers, and moped renters *(top, left)* *Twain Newhart*

Members of *Halau* Na Mamo'o Ka'ala complete their final costume preparations
before entertaining the crowd of Sunday shoppers at Ala Moana Center Stage *(top, right)*. *Susan Aimee Weinik*

A local mom helps her young son fashion the internationally recognized sign of *aloha (bottom, left)*. *David S. Boynton*

Musicians of the Royal Hawaiian Band pack up their instruments
following a Sunday afternoon concert at the Kapi'olani Park bandstand *(bottom, right)*. *Franco Salmoiraghi*

Green bubble eyes, pink bubble mouth *(top, left)*. San Diego Padres' first base coach, Davey Lopes, stands on the sidelines, sporting mean shades and a three-inch gum bubble. Could it be a signal to steal third?
Kirk Lee Aeder

⋅ ⋅ ⋅

"We brought you to the game. We bought you a balloon. You get to sit on *tutukane*'s lap. What more do you want?" *(top, right)*
Franco Salmoiraghi

⋅ ⋅ ⋅

On Mother's Day, the last game of the University of Hawai'i baseball season, Neal Honma swings, and hits one high and away for mom *(right)*. UH won that day.
Franco Salmoiraghi

⋅ ⋅ ⋅

The unsung heroes of America's favorite pastime smooth the dirt between the bases at Aloha Stadium during a San Diego Padres game *(below)*.
Kirk Lee Aeder

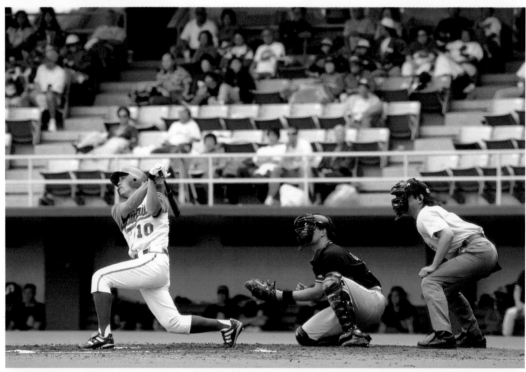

San Diego Padres fans stretch out among rows of empty seats *(above)*. Local crowds came to Aloha Stadium on this baseball Sunday to watch the first regular season major league game ever played in Hawai'i.
Kirk Lee Aeder

Layered with *lei* after their final game of the season, the University of Hawai'i Rainbow baseball team's five graduating seniors hold up their farewell banner *(left)*.
Franco Salmoiraghi

Body language says it all. A couple sorts out a scheduling problem on a bench in front of Boston Pizza on Waialae Avenue. He was supposed to meet her for lunch and was an hour late.
Ian Gillespie

"Cultural interchange has definite practical aspects in promoting peace and stability" *(Chancellor Howard P. Jones)*
Twain Newhart

HAROLD H. HIGASHIHARA PARK

DEPT. OF PARKS & RECREATION
COUNTY OF HAWAII

VOLUNTEER
SIGN-UP
BIG GREEN TENT

(all photos by G. Brad Lewis except: this page, middle right photo by Cat & Kevin Sweeney)

Volunteers *from both the* mauka *and* makai *communities of Kailua-Kona gather for the benefit of their* keiki. *Artists, masons, construction workers, and families gave their time and talents to build Kamakana Playground at the Harold H. Higashihara Park. Children, under the guidance of experienced artisians, resined the decorative woodwork while their parents helped assemble the larger pieces.   Located on the* makai *side of Kuakini Highway in Honalo, Kona, on property owned and managed by the Hawai'i State Department of Parks and Recreation, the site features a collection of wooden structures that ignite the imagination. World-renowned playground designer Robert Leathers created this masterpiece.   The ground covering, a new material called "fibar," was used to make the area wheelchair accessible, to cushion a fall from heights up to ten feet, and to reduce the incidence of puddles in high traffic areas. This product doesn't splinter and is made without the use of chemicals.   The park consists of a 37-foot castle with a tube-slide that winds and twists from a height of 15 feet; an octopus with steps and rope ladders; a sugar cane train; an amphitheater that seats 60-70 people; a sandbox; a tot lot for 3 to 5 year olds; a rendering of an ancient Hawaiian voyaging canoe; nooks and crannies for hiding; a telephone that connects the castle, train, and canoe; and the regular slides, swings, and teeter-totters found in parks around the world. The highlight of the playground will be a 17-foot cement sculpture of a humpback whale.*

A t this Sunday car wash in
Honolulu they'll clean your car for $5.00, wash your van for $6.00,
and hose you down for free *(top, left)*. *Ian Gillespie*

• • •

Sometimes being with your parrot pal
at your favorite spot is all a body needs *(top, right)*. *Ian Gillespie*

"Man's need for some degree of beauty and serenity becomes more desperate as our lives become more complex." *(Aaron Levine, O'ahu Development Conference) (previous page) Twain Newhart*

• • •

With a billowing halo of yellow nylon, this man controls the elements *(right)*. Pulling the strings of his destiny, he eases the speed and governs the direction of his descent onto the field during the Outrigger Hydrofest at Pearl Harbor. *Gary Hofheimer*

Well-heeled Sunday shoppers admire the
classic style of a designer's ensemble *(above, top)*. The upper level of Ala Moana's Center Court is a
favorite sanctuary from the bustling consumer traffic on the floors below. *Gary Hofheimer*

Clean fire engines go faster *(above, left)*. The firefighters of Station #7 in Waikiki,
uniformed and ready for any emergency, spend their Sunday shining the windows and
polishing the paint on their yellow chariot of ladders and hoses. *Franco Salmoiraghi*

"Work is love made visible." *(Kahlil Gibran) (above, right) Chris Mitts*

The crowd at the International Mountain Bike Challenge at Kualoa Ranch oohs and aahs at the acrobatic artistry of this high-flying cyclist *(above)*.
Twain Newhart

• • •

Competitors race through the winding chutes to the finish line in a smear of color *(right)*.
Franco Salmoiraghi

A cluster of cyclists burns up
the empty Sunday streets of Waikiki *(above, top)*. *Twain Newhart*

• • •

Before a backdrop of international flags and the green of the Koʻolaus, racers set their pace
on the uphill grade of Kualoa's mountain bike track *(above, left)*. *Franco Salmoiraghi*

• • •

Banking into the last spectacular leg of the race, these fast cyclists must have to
concentrate to keep their eyes on the track *(above, right)*. *Franco Salmoiraghi*

• • •

Warm sunlight bathes the iron-rich peaks above Holua Campground
in Haleakala crater *(following page)*. *Ray Mains*

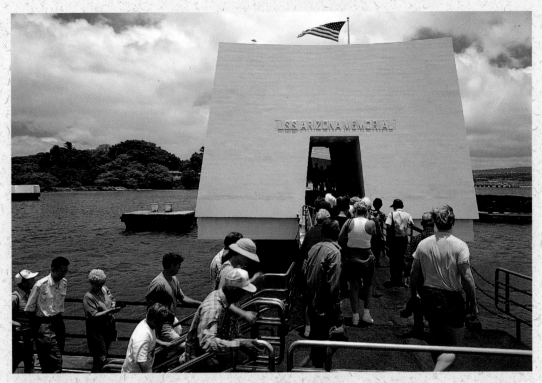

Hawai'i's strategic location makes it vital to the U.S. military. Headquartered at Pearl Harbor, the Commander-in-Chief Pacific (CINCPAC) oversees the largest command force on earth, covering the Pacific, Indian, and Arctic Oceans. Bases and training areas on O'ahu alone occupy 93,000 acres, 1/4 of the Island. The military is likewise vital to Hawai'i, employing thousands of residents across the state, and pumping billions of dollars into the local economy. For the Navy, Marine, Air Force, and Army personnel the Islands represent a dream assignment, even with Sunday duty. Balmy weather and blue skies make the toughest training exercises —like marching through the Ko'olau rain forests or practicing helicopter rescues —quite tolerable. The easier jobs range anywhere from office work to guard duty, to maintenance on the missile tubes of a Fast Attack Nuclear Submarine, to hosting tourists (as volunteer Everett Hyland, a survivor of the Pearl Harbor attack, does [above right]) at the U.S.S. Arizona Memorial. The military in laid-back Hawai'i represents a more disciplined, Spartan reality, a separate culture governed from afar. But its personnel and their families live, and laugh, and work with the rest of us, contributing a robust confluence of energies to our Island society.

In a straw hat with a
necktie band, a gateball player stands on the line of
opportunity and sets his shot *(above, left). Ron Dahlquist*

. . .

Sporting wristband scorekeepers and big numbered
buttons, members of the Kula Gateball Club meet every
Sunday for friendly competition and mallet-master's
bragging rights *(above, right). Ron Dahlquist*

Musician Jerry Santos and his Kiele Street friends (and Valentine, the dog) relax and play in the waning light of a Sunday afternoon. *Franco Salmoiraghi*

With the colors of embers anticipating the fire, Tahitian dancers' *i'i* wait for the swing and sway that will ignite them and thrill the hearts of the spectators *(opposite)*. G. Brad Lewis

. . .

Working with fire-heated river rocks and carefully placed *ti* leaves to line the open pit, local men labor as their ancestors did in the preparation of a traditional *imu (above)*. Native peoples throughout Polynesia used this efficient earth oven to cook their daily meals. Today, the ancient cooking technique blesses our holiday tables with savory *kalua* pig. Gary Hofheimer

. . .

"A good man doubles the length of his existence. To have lived so as to look back with pleasure is to have lived twice." *(Martial) (left)* G. Brad Lewis

. . .

After a heated Sunday match, this hardworking polo pony enjoys a cooling blast *(following page)*. Franco Salmoiraghi

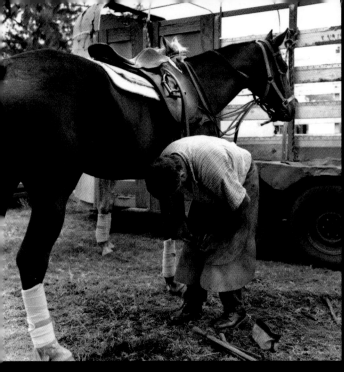

A polo pony gets a new set of
shoes before taking the field at Mokule'ia *(top, left)*. *Franco Salmoiraghi*

• • •

Before the polo match, fans stake out their tables at the Mokule'ia club house *(top, right)*. *Franco Salmoiraghi*

• • •

Between chukkars, spectators take their beverages onto the polo field and stamp in the divots
created by the pounding hoofs of the ponies *(bottom, left)*. Steaming divots
are naturally avoided. *Franco Salmoiraghi*

• • •

Polo fans are a friendly lot *(bottom, right)*. *Franco Salmoiraghi*

S tanding next to the goal at one
end of the Mokuleʻia field, this vitally important official collects and
cleans the game balls *(top, left)*. *Franco Salmoiraghi*

• • •

In this spectator sport of polo, the spectacle to be enjoyed is often in the crowd itself *(top, right)*.
Franco Salmoiraghi

• • •

Wine, bread, cheese, and a shoulder wrap
keep off the late afternoon chill *(bottom, left)*. *Franco Salmoiraghi*

• • •

Attending a polo match without wine would be unimaginable *(bottom, right)*. *Franco Salmoiraghi*

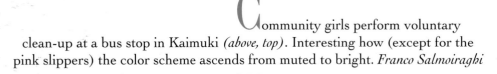

Community girls perform voluntary clean-up at a bus stop in Kaimuki *(above, top)*. Interesting how (except for the pink slippers) the color scheme ascends from muted to bright. *Franco Salmoiraghi*

• • •

She's not sure she's going to like how this tastes: a young girl watches a swap meet vendor scoop the meat out of a coconut *(above, bottom)*. *Chris Mitts*

• • •

Clouds of foam dust powder the shaping room of Bill Hamilton, who gets his creative inspiration from surfing the breaks near his home in Hanalei, Kaua'i *(opposite)*. For this 30-year veteran of surfboard manufacturing and design, it has to be a pretty flat Sunday to be out of the waves and into this unearthly get-up. *David S. Boynton*

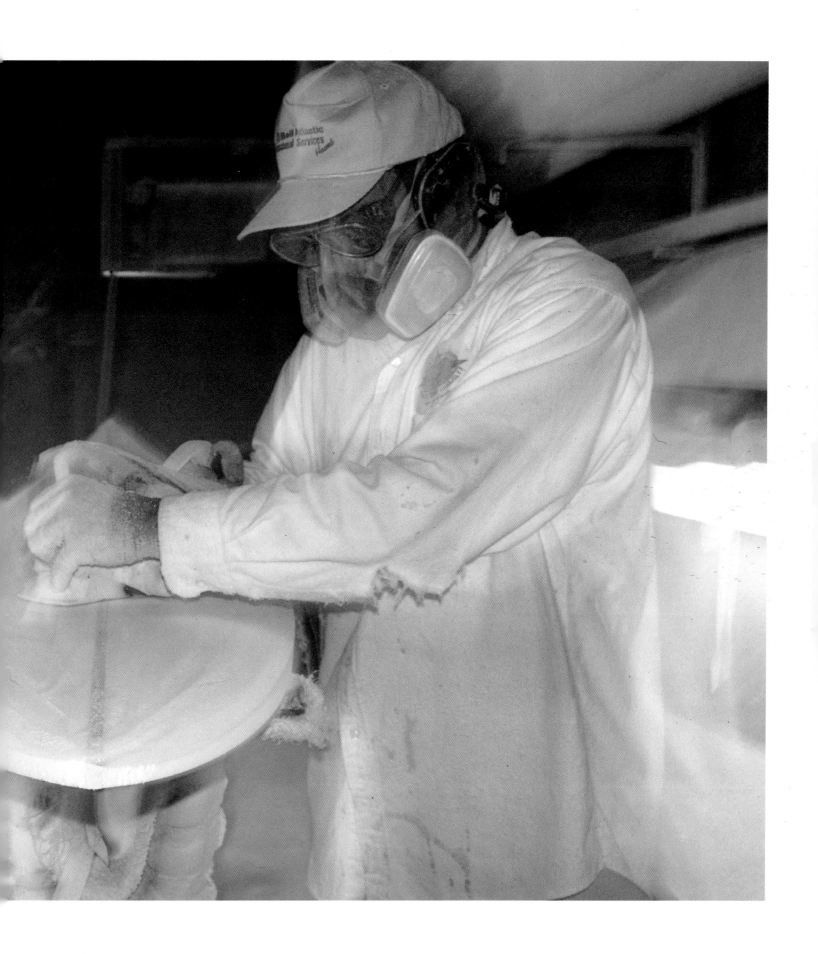

Life goes on.
Before a violent storm deposited
this hapless yacht on the lava outcropping,
the narrow strip of white sand was known as
Old Airport Beach *(above)*. Today, Kailua-Kona residents
have renamed the area Shipwreck Beach. They picnic
and play as they always have here, and tell stories
about the pretty hulk that is impossible
to salvage. *G. Brad Lewis*

· · ·

Safe in the hands of La'amaomao,
the Hawaiian goddess of winds, a hang-glider lifts off
from the Makapu'u cliff ramp into the double blue of sea
and sky *(above, opposite)*. *Lauren Lavonne Pritchett*

· · ·

Thundering down a Big Island road:
a small body on large wheels and a large body on small
wheels *(below, opposite)*. *G. Brad Lewis*

*F*or every
balloon there's a story.
Someone's feet hurt,
someone's having trouble
untangling a ribbon, and
someone just wants to go
back to Sunday shopping
at the Disney Store.
Susan Aimee Weinik

Pikake blossoms cascade from
her shoulders like a waterfall in a forest of *maile (top, left)*. The May Day queen at
Honaunau School on the Big Island leads a royal *hula*. *Cat & Kevin Sweeney*

It takes local florists in Upcountry Maui days to renew their stock
of blossoms following a Seabury School graduation *(top, right)*. *Ray Mains*

There's love in that look and artful detail in every aspect of the lives
of these two watercolorists—from the melon umbrella and *aloha* print garb to their paintings
displayed on the Sunday "Art Fence" at Honolulu Zoo *(bottom, left)*. *Chris Mitts*

A pink bouquet at the Pink Palace *(bottom, right)*. Japanese newlyweds ascend the arched entry
of the Royal Hawaiian Hotel, fulfilling a romantic dream shared by millions of young lovers. *Susan Aimee Weinik*

Graham Ellis, a Hilo resident, gathers his troop of circus performers for Sunday instruction on the beach at Spencer Beach Park *(previous page)*. Mr. Ellis teaches people of the community the fun arts of juggling, clowning, and unicycle antics. This group also features several international jugglers attending Graham's annual juggling convention.
G. Brad Lewis

• • •

A Sunday matinee crowd exits the landmark Hawaiʻi Theater (under renovation) in downtown Honolulu following an Iona Pear modern dance concert *(right)*.
Franco Salmoiraghi

The only person in this shot who looks crazy for anyone is the daddy for his little girl standing on the bench. But Diamond Head boasts a legion of loyal patrons who seem crazy about every show staged in this venerable old playhouse. *Franco Salmoiraghi*

• • •

In a festival of international cultures at the University of Hawai'i's East-West Center, a mother acquaints her little ones with the costumes of India *(left)*. The dot or jewel worn in the center of the forehead, considered a sign of beauty by Indian women, is called a *kumkum*.
Franco Salmoiraghi

151

"Music! man's music, and yet so much
more than man! The last unfolding of breathless hope!" *(Jorge Guillen)* *(top, left) Richard A. Cooke, III.*

• • •

Emi Azeka Preston, a member of George Allen's painting class *(top, right)*, does a pallet-knife rendition
of the Hui No'eau Visual Arts Center in the little community of Makawao in Upcountry, Maui. *Ron Dahlquist*

• • •

His lips pursed round with concentration, a boccie ball enthusiast sets himself for the toss *(bottom, left)*.
This traditional Italian sport, played with wooden balls, brings Honolulu's Italian community
out for Sunday games. *Susan Aimee Weinik*

• • •

With a skillful balance of tension and subtle movement *(bottom, right)*, Kaua'i's
nationally renowned woodworker Bob Hamada lathes a pheasant-wood bowl. *David S. Boynton*

152

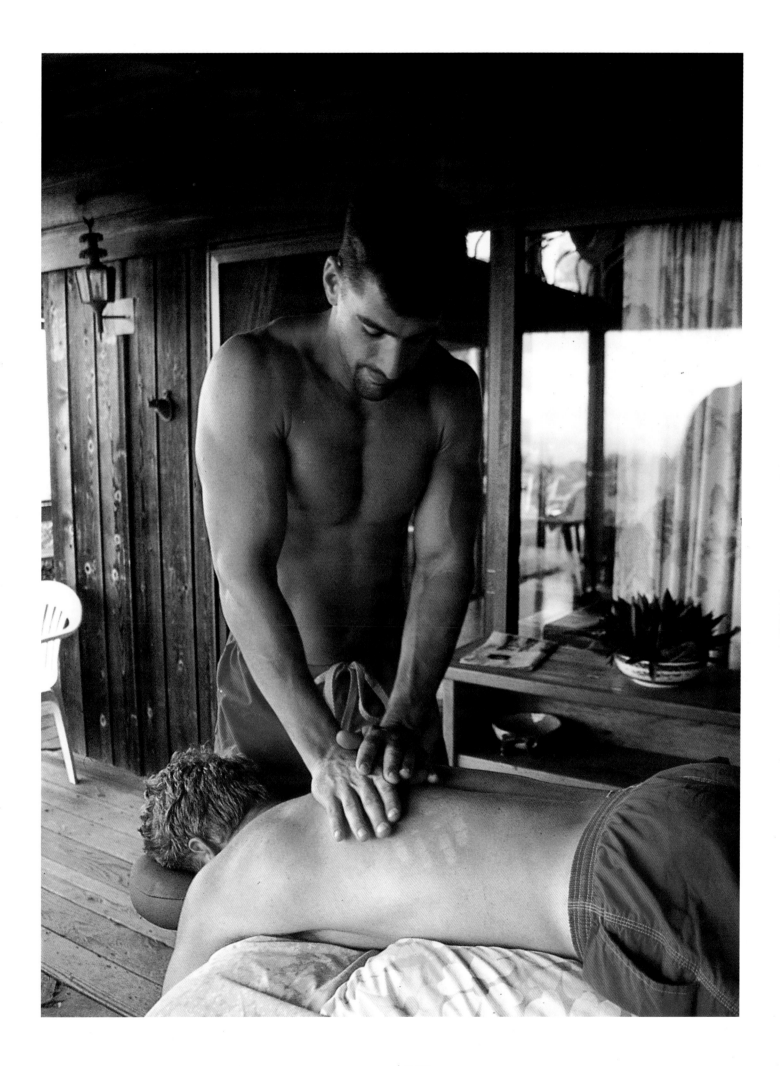

A sibling chiropractic
adjustment *(previous page)* on Sunday-sunburned skin
leaves the handmark of the doctor: Blake and Brett
James on their Moloka'i *lanai. Bronwyn Cooke*

· · ·

Each year the crowd gets bigger
at the Sunday finals of the Pipeline Masters
surf competion. *Gary Hofheimer*

A proud young mom shades her baby from the noonday sun in Kapi'olani Park at the 24th International Bed Race festivities *(top)*. *Franco Salmoiraghi*

· · ·

A healthy family of three zips by on a bicycle built for two *(middle, top)*. *Twain Newhart*

· · ·

On Sunday, April 17, 1997, lucky anglers at Honokohau Harbor in Kailua-Kona string up and weigh their catch *(middle, bottom)*. That's a yellow-fin tuna *(ahi)* on the scale, a ten-pounder *(awa 'aua)* in the middle, and a dark blue *hauliuli* to the left. All three are excellent tasting pelagic fishes. *G. Brad Lewis*

· · ·

A variety of cloth hats and cameras point toward Maui's 'Iao Needle *(bottom)*. On this particular Sunday, as her tour mates jockey for the best picture, one of the women has flipped her hippopotamus around so the large brim won't disturb her shot. *Ron Dahlquist*

Hawai'i's premier *hula* competition *(above)*, the Merrie Monarch, begins with a festive *ho'olaulea* at Coconut Island in Hilo. Dance and musical groups (like these Tahitian drummers) from around the Pacific gather the Sunday before the week-long activities to perform at this classic celebration of Island heritage. *G. Brad Lewis*

· · ·

Dressed in a layered *malo (right)*, a dancer of the *halau* Kawaili'ula, bends with arms *akimbo* imitating the flapping walk of a bird. *Ray Mains*

· · ·

You can see the family resemblance in these bright brown eyes on a brown sand beach on Moloka'i *(above, opposite)*. *Richard A. Cooke, III.*

· · ·

Gay Wong and her family celebrate Mother's Day Sunday *(below, opposite)* with a 10-course luncheon at Hee Hing's Chinese Restaurant in Honolulu. With an enticing dangle of noodles, Gay tells her little niece to "open wide like a baby bird." *Susan Aimee Weinik*

Before an ancient lichen-speckled enclosure wall *(previous page)*, a young Hawaiian woman helps her *kukuhine* along the rocky path of the coconut grove on the hallowed grounds of Pu'uhonuna O Honaunau on the Big Island.
Bronwyn Cooke

• • •

A local family, all set up for a day at Twelve Palms Beach across Kalakaua Avenue from Kapi'olani Park, poses for a casual group shot *(above, opposite)*.
Susan Aimee Weinik

• • •

A pair of visitors strolls past a friendly Sunday game of horseshoes in a Waikiki park as a player aims for a ringer *(below left, opposite)*.
Susan Aimee Weinik

• • •

Activities that qualify as Sunday relaxation are as varied as the sands on the beach. After putting their tired *keiki* down for a nap, mom and aunties settle in for a relaxing game of cribbage *(below right, opposite)*.
Susan Aimee Weinik

• • •

Even in the solemnity of Nature's green and golden cathedrals, there may be cause for hilarious laughter *(left)*.
G. Brad Lewis

• • •

In Sunday sunshine for Saturday's clothes *(following page)*, a little girl gently pulls a shirt from the laundry basket so as not to dislodge Mommy's portable phone. *Sri Maiva Rusden*

For some, Sunday is the only day during their busy week that Hawai'i's people can contribute items to their favorite charity *(above, opposite)*. Salvation Army accepts donations from anyone, anytime.
Franco Salmoiraghi

• • •

A Sunday fund-raiser car-wash is a lot more fun than you'd ever imagine, under gray skies that promise more customers on Kaua'i *(below left, opposite)*.
David S. Boynton

• • •

Honolulu International Airport explodes with traffic, luggage, and fond embraces every Sunday afternoon *(below right, opposite)*. *Twain Newhart*

• • •

Daddy stands close and watches as these young night riders *(left)*, clinging to the poles of their carousel ponies, experience the slightly scary spin of a merry-go-round.
Chris Mitts

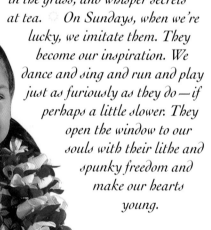

Hawaii's keiki —
all smiles and full of kolohe mischief. Their eyes mirror our youth. In them lie the dreams from our past, and the hopes for their future. Our children mimic us when they string lei, play sports, hang out with friends, and cheese it up for the camera. Or when they help each other at the water fountain, or dance the legends and stories of Hawai'i's ancestors.   Our best expression of aloha shines through our keiki with the freshness of a Sunday morning. They love watermelon, and bubbles, and a cold bath in a tin tub. They love hiding under an umbrella or table, climbing trees, sharing sand, and waving good-bye. They look for fish under bridges, give happy hula hugs, ride unicycles in the grass, and whisper secrets at tea.   On Sundays, when we're lucky, we imitate them. They become our inspiration. We dance and sing and run and play just as furiously as they do — if perhaps a little slower. They open the window to our souls with their lithe and spunky freedom and make our hearts young.

(opposite page — from top, left to right: Sri Maiava Rusden, Ray Mains, Ron Dahlquist, Brett Uprichard, Ron Dahlquist; this page — from top, left to right: G. Brad Lewis, David S. Boynton, Kirk Lee Aeder, Ray Mains)

(from top, left to right: David S. Boynton, G. Brad Lewis, Susan Aimee Weinik, Bronwyn Cooke, Ray Mains, G. Brad Lewis, Kirk Lee Aeder)

(from top, left to righ: G. Brad Lewis, Margo Berdeshevsky, G. Brad Lewis, Richard A. Cooke, III., Susan Aimee Weinik, Susan Aimee Weinik)

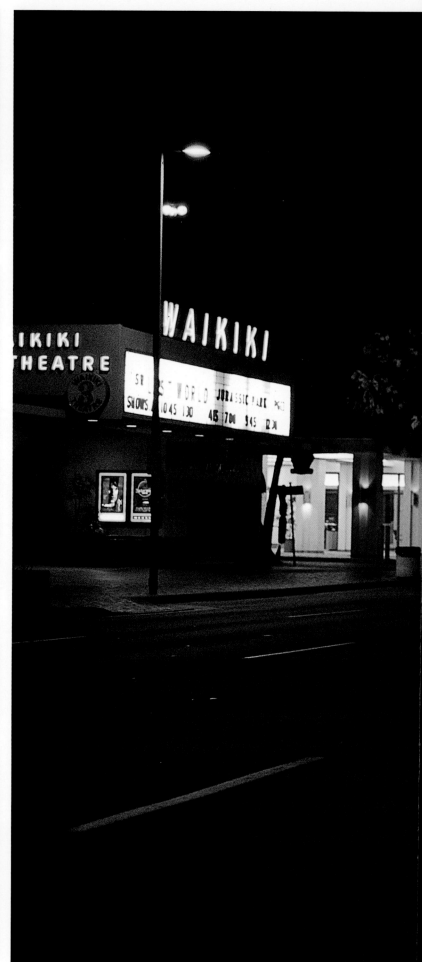

One weekend a year *(previous page)*, when the goddess Poli'ahu dresses her mountain, Mauna Kea, in a cloak of snow, young snowboarders test their aerial acrobatics against a backdrop of futuristic, domed observatories and ice-crusted lava. *Kirk Lee Aeder*

• • •

As they glide through a pool of light *(top, opposite)*, these dancers in the Chinese Phoenix Dance Concert at Diamond Head Theater, betray none of the frantic hours spent backstage preparing for this golden moment. *Franco Salmoiraghi*

• • •

A trio of raucus singers pounds out a red-hot number of song and dance on platform shoes *(middle top, opposite)*, at the evening's entertainment for the 24th International Bed Race. *Franco Salmoiraghi*

• • •

"Wow! Can you dance!" An eager photographer rushes from a crowd to request a picture of a young, blushing *hula* maiden *(middle bottom, opposite)*. *Susan Aimee Weinik*

• • •

Sunday mornings are usually slow for "Honolulu's finest." Either way, the door to the Waikiki Police Substation on Kalakaua Avenue is always open *(bottom, opposite)*. *Twain Newhart*

• • •

In the pre-dawn darkness after Saturday's revelers have gone to bed *(left)*, Waikiki's busy thoroughfare, Kalakaua Avenue, rests. *Twain Newhart*

F itness guru
Gil Janklowicz *(top, left)* plans out his keynote address before
the opening ceremony of the Isreali Independence Day festivities at Kapi'olani Park. *Susan Aimee Weinik*

From pizza to spirituality *(top, right)*, the booths
offer a fascinating range of sustenance. *Susan Aimee Weinik*

Under the flamboyant tutelage of the Hawai'i Israeli Recreational Dance Troop
children learn the traditional dances of their Hebrew heritage *(bottom, left)*. *Susan Aimee Weinik*

A Snapple salesman advertises his wares at the Pita King booth *(bottom, right)*. *Susan Aimee Weinik*

Gil Janklowicz strains
a look at some savory pita sandwiches *(top, left)*. *Susan Aimee Weinik*

• • •

The young volunteers for Chabad of Hawai'i smile for the camera *(top, right)*. *Susan Aimee Weinik*

With brushes in hand and paint landing everywhere *(bottom, left)* —
on themselves, their clothes, each other, and the canvas—these beautiful little girls compose
a masterpiece that rivals the work of famous abstract artists. *Susan Aimee Weinik*

• • •

The chefs of the Pita King Restaurant serve up some meaty wraps
at the Israeli Independence Day celebration at Kapi'olani Park *(bottom, right)*. *Susan Aimee Weinik*

A powerful Papa propels his boy into a shorebreak wave on a *kiawe*-lined strip of beach on Moloka'i *(above)*. *Richard A. Cooke, III.*

· · ·

Topped with strings of Ni'ihau shells and polished coconut cups, a *hula* dancer on the Big Island receives a costume adjustment from her friend *(right)*. *G. Brad Lewis*

· · ·

Using her hand as an air-rudder *(above, opposite)*, this young girl does the best she can to help her dad steer through a Sunday comber at The Wall Kapahulu groin at Waikiki. *Lauren Lavonne Pritchett*

· · ·

In waters shallow enough for a helping hand, diver Matt Sweeney experiences first contact with the reefs while visiting his Big Island family *(below, opposite)*. *Cat & Kevin Sweeney*

A chip-shot to glory:
a pro at the Kaʻanapali Senior Golf Classic follows his
shot toward the cup *(left)*. See the ball? *Ray Mains*

• • •

An expert putter triumphantly plucks out
a ball that gave him a birdie *(right)*. *Ray Mains*

• • •

Young Dillon McCall does a flying header
at soccer practice at Eddie Tam Field in Makawao,
Upcountry Maui *(previous page)*. *Ron Dahlquist*

"You know,
I can't tell if this ball is stuck in a water hazard or in the
rough." *(left) Ray Mains*

• • •

Four eyes are better than two: a pro and his caddie
consult the contours *(right). Ray Mains*

• • •

Pro Beach Volleyball will never find a better court than
this one, on the most famous beach in the world *(following
page)*. Shot from the Hilton Hawaiian Village, over the
Fort DeRussy section of Waikiki Beach.
Lauren Lavonne Pritchett

(from top, left to right: Ray Mains, G. Brad Lewis, Susan Aimee
Weinik, Ray Mains, Ray Mains, Ron Dahlquist)

F or being "The Crossroads of the Pacific," Hawai'i manifests a society not so wildly eccentric as you might expect. Still, we are blessed with an assortment of quixotic characters more than willing to fight the good fight against the windmills of the mundane. ☼ There's a kind of fearlessness of individuality among Hawai'i's people. We think nothing of flying flamboyant kites, or of making business calls from a lu'au, or wearing funny hats, or funny shoes — or wearing stilts and throwing juggling batons into the air — or brushing our teeth out in the open, keeping company with pigeons, or of making public displays of who we are and what we love: pink princesses at the Pink Palace, for instance. ☼ Hawai'i is the best show going, its population is the happiest cast of actors alive, and Sunday, it seems, is our weekly grand finale.

(from top, left to right: Susan Aimee Weinik, Chris Mitts, Susan Aimee Weinik, Richard A. Cooke, III.)

Before each sham fight in the Sunday martial arts classes at the Nigashi Hong Wanji Mission *(top left, opposite)*, opponents bow to each other in a sign of respect. *Franco Salmoiraghi*

• • •

In Aikido, students learn how to throw an attacker by using his own aggressive force against him *(top right, opposite)*. *Franco Salmoiraghi*

• • •

An Aikido master checks the technique of his students throughout the practice *(bottom, opposite)*. *Franco Salmoiraghi*

• • •

The quickness of a fall defies normal shutter speed on a camera *(bottom right, opposite)*. *Franco Salmoiraghi*

• • •

"This is my favorite part of class, where we get to stand and laugh while everybody else has to knock each other around." *(above) Franco Salmoiraghi*

• • •

The strategy of a good grip is what wins a match *(left, top and bottom)*. *Franco Salmoiraghi*

Τhe weekend concludes
with a sunset over the 50th State Fair in the Aloha Stadium parking lot
(opposite), where any of these glowing carnival rides could be
called the "Ring of Fire." *Twain Newhart*

· · ·

By special request, hairstylist Richard Shaedon of the Panache salon in Kaimuki
occasionally opens his shop on Sunday for VIP customers *(above, top)*. Richard's son
Taurean, his dad's personal VIP, gets a trendy trim. *Julie Sotomura*

· · ·

Old rock drummers never die they just play polo *(above, bottom)*,
and occasionally sit in with the Sunday band at the Mokule'ia Polo Field—like this
gentleman: Ginger Baker, former drummer of Cream. *Franco Salmoiraghi*

Lahainalua High School students
get the thrill of a lifetime on a brisk Sunday afternoon aboard the *Moʻolele (opposite)*, a
Maui-built replica of an ancient double-hulled Hawaiian voyaging canoe. *Ron Dahlquist*

✳ ✳ ✳

As the day wears on one young seafarer wears out *(above, top)*, while her companion
attempts to steer. *Ron Dahlquist*

✳ ✳ ✳

The *Moʻolele* tacks through a cross-swell off Maui's Kaʻanapali coast *(above, bottom)*.
Ron Dahlquist

✳ ✳ ✳

The Waikiki Acrobatic Troop practices every Sunday afternoon to the delight of
beachgoers *(previous page)*. *Franco Salmoiraghi*

With their shoes removed, and some of them
sitting on soda-can cardboard, members of a local Buddist temple settle into a Sunday picnic at
Ala Moana Beach Park. *Chris Mitts*

Self-portrait in convex
dark glasses: the photographer sees what his subject
sees in this reflective panarama of a canoe race on
Kaua'i's Wailua River *(top, left)*. *David S. Boynton*

• • •

Wearing her cool, Island-style lawn-mowing
ensemble of hat, bikini-top, *pareau*, and rubber boots, Sue
Boynton takes a Sunday turn around her Kaua'i yard
(top, right). *David S. Boynton*

• • •

Sister Richard Marie, "the fishing nun," celebrated
her 60th anniversary of service to the Catholic church
with a Diamond Jubilee service at Kalaupapa on
Moloka'i, where she has lived and worked
for the past 35 years *(left)*.
Richard A. Cooke, III.

Hawai'i's governor hosts a dinner party to honor Israel's Ambassador to the United States. Left to right: Governor Ben Cayetano, Lieutenant Governor Mazie Hirono, the governor's wife, Vicki Liu Cayetano, Mrs. Elissar, and the Israeli Ambassador, Eliahu Ben Elissar, at the governor's mansion, Washington Place *(above)*. *Susan Aimee Weinik*

⋅ ⋅ ⋅

Harpist Ruth Freedman plucks a sequence of heavenly chords *(right)*. *Susan Aimee Weinik*

⋅ ⋅ ⋅

In the shadow of the ridge-top cross at Punchbowl, with bougainvillea blossoms shining below, news photographer Cory Lum searches for his shot of the Easter sunrise service *(previous page)*. *Franco Salmoiraghi*

A tastefully dressed
State Representative visits a group of dignitaries on the
verandah *(above)*. *Susan Aimee Weinik*

· · ·

Govenor Cayetano takes a quiet moment to study his
notes before delivering a welcome speech to the
Ambassador and guests *(following page)*.
Susan Aimee Weinik

Big Island artists *(above)*, who have left behind their easels and writing to hike the heights of Nature's creation, pose on the chilly summit of Mauna Loa.
G. Brad Lewis

• • •

The great thing about a kids' Sunday School is all the cute little faces *(left)*, as in this class at Keawali Congregational Church in Makena on Maui.
Ron Dahlquist

(page 202-205 photos by Franco Salmoiraghi)

H-3, America's most expensive stretch of road, has cost more than just tax dollars. It towers over and runs through significant archeological sites in the valleys of Halawa (above Pearl City) and Ha'iku and Luluku on windward O'ahu. ❀ From its conception through its imminent completion, the highway has divided the people of Hawai'i along political, racial, and cultural lines. ❀ On April 20, 1997, before the road was ready to open for automobile traffic, organizers held the Great Trans-Ko'olau Race (the one-time 10K Sunday "fun-run" starting in Kane'ohe and ending at Aloha Stadium). ❀ Protesters with signs and Hawaiian flags shouted their disapproval as the runners arrived in buses at the Kane'ohe starting line. Race promoters advertised an anticipated field of 100,000. Only 17,000 signed up to tour the controversial freeway. They filled the lanes and corridors of concrete with a river of dotted color. ❀ "It's done, and I bet everyone will drive on it," said one runner, standing with her son. "I just wanted something fun to do with my boy, so we're here." ❀ After the boom of the starting cannon — fired by the Hawai'i National Guard 487th Field Artillery Group — the racers began to stretch out along the route, their attention turned from the shouts to the quiet miles of mountains and   trees ahead.

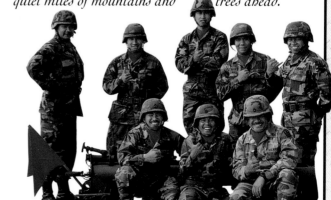

Hot Sunday speed: Hawai'i
Raceway Park features the state's only drag strip and automobile race course
(opposite). Although races are rare on Sunday (Saturday being the prime race day),
car freaks savor every opportunity to watch these earth-bound
rockets blow. *Twain Newhart*

* * *

Jeff, the dog trainer *(above, top)*,
works with his clients and their masters. *Franco Salmoiraghi*

* * *

Badgered by his birds *(above, bottom)*, Robert Rushworth hand-feeds the merchandise
at the Aina Haina Home & Garden Center in Kaimuki. He was a little reluctant to
have one on his head. He says that when a bird is perched above you, it thinks it
rules the roost. *Franco Salmoiraghi*

No one smiles like
newlyweds *(opposite)*. A young Japanese couple,
just sealed in holy matrimony, heads for their
limousine and Waikiki. *Sri Maiava Rusden*

• • •

Enjoying a Sunday afternoon
in the shade by the canal *(above)*, Mom
is prepared for any suprises from the
branches above. *Twain Newhart*

Their backs bright with sweat *(top, left)*,
local boys transport *kalua* pig from the *imu* to the tables of waiting *luʻau* guests. *G. Brad Lewis*

Good, thick *poi* is one-finger *poi*: *Ai Poi* (*poi* tasting)
ceremony at Hana's Au I Na Kai ʻEwalu gathering *(top, right)*. *Ray Mains*

It's not clear why a manhole sits in the middle of a lovely park *(bottom, right)*,
but this young man has found good use for the cover. He claims to make "da mos' ono-est"
barbecued teriyaki and chicken in Hawaiʻi. *Franco Salmoiraghi*

Representing three generations of one family, four ladies sample
the Mother's Day brunch buffet at the Royal Hawaiian Hotel. *(bottom, left) Susan Aimee Weinik*

The
captain receives an
appreciative hug for this
Sunday sail through the
shimmering deep-blue
waters off the Big Island.
G. Brad Lewis

211

*A*uthor Glen Grant
strikes a pose in the guise of a 1930s detective *(above)*, his
costume as a tour guide to mysterious sites in downtown
Honolulu. *Ian Gillespie*

• • •

"Double-cross" takes on a benign new meaning in the
play of light and shadows at this lonely cemetery cabin on
Kalaupapa peninsula, Moloka'i *(right)*.
Richard A. Cooke, III.

212

"Execute every act of thy life as though it were thy last." *(Marcus Aurelius) (top photos) Twain Newhart*

. . .

"So then—" "Yeah?" "The crab said, 'Pinch me!'" "Oh, ha ha ha ha ha!" "I love the way you laugh." *(bottom photos) Gregg Alan Sonmore*

. . .

All of life, like the sea, is a flow. And in the ballet of net throwing we must understand that flow as the fish do. Only then will our nets be full. *(opposite) Gregg Alan Sonmore*

"No one knows what he can do till he tries, and tries again." *(Publilius Syrus)* On a Moloka'i country road a skateboarder jumps and twirls through a choreography born out of the pure love of motion. He still can't shake his blue jeans off. *Richard A. Cooke, III.*

Mom and the kids go fishing for treasure
at a Sunday fair *(top, left)*. Children who believe in Santa Claus and the Easter Bunny
have no problem expecting to magically hook some goodies from cardboard waves. *Franco Salmoiraghi*

• • •

A couple of basketball stars ham it up with the Little Mermaid
at a children's fair in Kapiʻolani Park *(top, right)*. *Franco Salmoiraghi*

• • •

In a valley along Makiki Heights at the Hawaiʻi Nature Center *(bottom, left)*, gloved volunteers
remove a leafy string of "cat's claw" vine, a nuisance plant considered one of the strongest botanical threats
to Island rain forests. *Franco Salmoiraghi*

• • •

Dog owners show off their precious babies after obedience
training class in Kamamalu Park in Nuʻuanu Valley *(bottom, right)*. *Franco Salmoiraghi*

Each branch of the
U.S. military—Army, Air Force, Navy, Marines—is
represented in this marching color guard *(above, top)*.
Gary Hofheimer

* * *

Packing the newest innovations in *faux* firepower
(following page), the dedicated warriors of Island Paintball
Sport line up for Sunday target practice at their new
Bellows Field course. *Franco Salmoiraghi*

Dancers make a limbo bar
out of their arms while local entertainer Henry Kapono sings calypso *(above, top)*.
Julie Sotomura

• • •

At the "meet shop," everyone's either making or planning their moves *(above, bottom)*.
Julie Sotomura

• • •

A waitress, at the Duke's Bar and Grill Sunday
bash in Waikiki, carries through the crowd a tray of unholy grails *(opposite)*.
Julie Sotomura

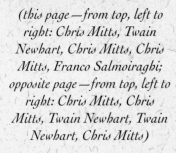

(this page—from top, left to right: Chris Mitts, Twain Newhart, Chris Mitts, Chris Mitts, Franco Salmoiraghi; opposite page—from top, left to right: Chris Mitts, Chris Mitts, Twain Newhart, Twain Newhart, Chris Mitts)

W here's everybody gone? Downtown Honolulu's notorious traffic that clogs the streets six days a week, miraculously drains away on Sunday. From the lavendar of sunrise to the warm orange of dusk, the quiet tranquillity of this empty cityscape resonates only with a memory of last week's buzz of big business. A car, a solitary jogger, or a lone cyclist owns the avenues of this temporary ghost town. Without the usual distractions, it's a great way to view Honolulu's dramatic architecture. As with any great cosmopolitan city, you catch glimpses of yester- day and tomorrow around every corner. The quaint old buildings date back to the Hawaiian Monarchy. The newest glass towers have yet to settle on their concrete- pile foundations. The unfettered views in these images include historic Murphy's Bar and Grill on the corner of Nu'uanu and Merchant, the shimmering monoliths of the financial district, the palm tree-inspired columns of the State Capitol building, the mall gardens and plazas, tree-shrouded St. Andrew's Cathedral, and the bell tower of Honolulu Hale (City Hall).

Local beachboys at Waikiki Beach
kick back and relax after a day of surf lessons and canoe rides *(top, left)*. *Susan Aimee Weinik*

· · ·

There's so much to see at the Contemporary Museum *(top, right)*, on Makiki Heights Drive
overlooking Honolulu, that you might lose your focus swirling from one stunning exibit to the next. *Franco Salmoiraghi*

· · ·

Puny pugilists stand ready for their first lessons in Thai kick-boxing *(bottom, left)*, at the
Loy Krathong Festival (held during the full moon of the twelfth lunar cycle). *Brett Uprichard*

· · ·

Eschewing the fanfare and spectacle of a traditional wedding *(bottom, right)*, this couple
takes their vows before a pastor (for validity), a photographer (for posterity), and God. *G. Brad Lewis*

Smoking and cycling, bad for you good for you: a barefoot denizen of the Ala Wai Yacht Harbor in Waikiki cruises around the slips.
Twain

In high spirits before the big game, a Sunday seniors' softball team smiles for the camera at War Memorial Fields on Maui *(previous page)*. *Ron Dahlquist*

• • •

Participants in the Honolulu Marathon flow bumper-to-bumper through the early phases of the race *(opposite)*. *Twain Newhart*

• • •

Waiting their turn in the next heat, members of the U.S. Army's 45th Corp Support Group cheer on fellow 24th Honolulu International Bed Race teams *(above)*. *Franco Salmoiraghi*

• • •

Passersby admire a painting of Pele's fountains *(left)*, an artistic adaptation of a famous photo by G. Brad Lewis, hung on the Sunday Art Fence at Honolulu Zoo. It's hard to believe this urban garden lies only 200 miles north of active Kilauea Volcano. *Franco Salmoiraghi*

• • •

Sunday morning laundry drapes the porch on an old plantation house *(following page)*. In Hana, on the rain-drenched windward coast of Maui, clothes are hung to dry under the eaves. *Ray Mains*

Sunday patrons retire to Coffee Time's
air conditioned dining room for a game of chess over glasses of iced tea *(top, left)*, or
cappuccino and conversation at the bar. *Ian Gillespie*

· · ·

A man bows his head *(middle, left)*, maybe to pray for help with this amazingly helpless hand,
or to hide a fading poker-face, or to catch a little nap as the other card players labor over their strategies. *Ian Gillespie*

· · ·

His beloved skateboard parked where he can keep an eye on it, a young player faces the challenge
of a chess board *(bottom, left)*. *Chris Mitts*

· · ·

Kuhio Park's kings of the cards bring along their own
hand-stitched table cloth *(right)*. *Chris Mitts*

With his opponent's rapt gaze reflected in his dark glasses *(left)*, a seasoned veteran of the chess wars presses home his attack.
Julie Sotomura

• • •

"Each time, Honolulu city lights bring me back again." *(Keola and Kapono Beamer) (following page)*
Franco Salmoiraghi

• • •

Sunsets on Sunday are no more golden than on any other day, it's just that there are more golden moments to enjoy them.
(following page)
Franco Salmoiraghi

Sunday In Hawai'i *assignment photographers, from left to right: Richard A. Cooke, III., David S. Boynton, Bronwyn Cooke, Ron Dahlquist, Franco Salmoiraghi, G. Brad Lewis, Julie Sotomura.*

*M*ost of the photographs for Sunday In Hawai'i *were shot on assignment during the warm, vivid Sundays of April and May. Many of the images reflect a preconceived list, what we thought might work within the theme of the book. But assignments sometimes prove constrictive, and we asked the photographers to feel free on this very free day to shoot whatever else attracted them, what seemed magical beyond the photo list. ✿ We asked that they remember to take the shots only on Sunday and that they shift their cameras away from the luminous landscapes that make up most picture books in the Islands, and focus instead on Hawai'i's people. ✿ They responded with an assortment of extraordinary images beyond anything we could have imagined.*

Kirk Lee Aeder finds living in hot and barren Waikoloa ideal for his work because it's in the center of the **Big Island**, and he can move quickly to locations. His photos reflect such alacrity, with water sports his specialty, although he has shot pro football and baseball on the mainland as well. His publications include *Fodor's Exploring Hawaii, Outside, Surfer, Endless Vacation* magazine, *Hawai'i* magazine, *Aloha*, and *Sports Illustrated.*

An acclaimed writer as well as photographer, **Margo Berdeshevsky** won the 1997 grand prize in the Borders Books/Honolulu magazine fiction contest. She exhibits her photos, often accompanied by her poems, in Island galleries and internationally, most recently at the Maui Arts and Cultural Center. Gallery Maui in Makawao has her limited edition

photos on current view. She travels often from her home on the north coast of **Maui**, to document local practices and controversies, and champion the Hawaiian cause. She also co-authored a limited edition book handmade in Indonesia called *Angel Heirs.*

David Boynton was born and raised on O'ahu, and moved to **Kaua'i** in 1974 to teach science at Waimea High School. He lives with his wife Sue Boynton and two stepdaughters at river's edge in Hanalei, and they also have a cabin in Koke'e State Park, where David teaches environmental resources at Koke'e Discovery Center. His photography has appeared in numerous local and national publications, and his landscape images illustrated the *Kaua'i Movie Book* (1996). Regarded as one of Kaua'i's best

photographers and educators, David takes his inspiration from the Island's spectacular natural environment.

Richard A. Cooke, III. lives on the old family ranch on **Moloka'i** with his wife **Bronwyn** (whose photography also appears in *Sunday In Hawai'i*). Richard has worked for 15 years with the National Geographic Society as a freelance photographer. His books include *Moloka'i: An Island in Time* (with Bronwyn), *The Blueridge Range, America's Ancient Cities*, and the *Smithsonian Guide to Natural America — Hawaii*, as well as chapters and other assignments for the National Geographic Society. He also does work nationally for Hyatt, Hilton, and other resorts, and locally for Bank of Hawai'i and the Moloka'i Ranch Limited.

Ron Dahlquist, rarely without his camera, has built a stock

library of over 60,000 images in 30 years of professional photography. *Life, Time, National Geographic, Forbes, Esquire, Islands, Family Fun, Conde Nast Traveler, Powder, Ski, Surfer, Snowboarder,* and *Windsurfer* have published his work, and *Runner's World, Outside, Aloha, Islands of Aloha,* and *Guest Informant* recently selected his shots for covers. Ron lives with his partner and wife Sharon and son Scott in the windsurfing mecca of Pa'ia, and specializes in capturing sports action and landscapes on **Maui**, and in worldwide travel. He holds several travel journalism awards. The coffeetable books *Maui Bound, Under a Maui Sun,* and *Maui* also carry Ron Dahlquist covers, and the beautiful travel guide *The Valley Isle* features his photos exclusively.

Ian Gillespie is a new talent in

Hawai'i photography. This O'ahu native and graduate of the School of the Art Institute of Chicago (where he studied painting, photography, and filmmaking) has exhibited abstract paintings, sculptures, and furniture at the Sìsu Gallery, Ché Pasta, the Honolulu Art Academy, and various galleries in Chicago. *Sunday In Hawai'i* marks Ian's debut in a volume of photo-journalism.

Gary Hofheimer lives at Sunset Beach on **O'ahu**, and operates the Honolulu-based Gary Hofheimer Photography, specializing in advertising and corporate communications as well as editorial. Gary's photos have appeared in the magazines *Honolulu, Pacific Business News,* and *Aloha,* and in the Mutual book *Architecture in Hawai'i—A Chronological Survey.*

Internationally recognized as a leading volcano photographer, **G. Brad Lewis** lives on the **Big Island,** in a coconut grove above a black sand beach on the flank of Kilauea, the most active volcano on earth. His stunning lava flow images have appeared on the covers of *Life, GEO, Natural History, Honolulu,* and within the pages of *National Geographic, Time, Newsweek, Outside, New York Times, Islands, Summit, Omni, Earth, Outdoor Photographer, Sunset, Forbes,* and many others. His nature images are used in advertising, books, calendars and stock. His fine art prints "LAVART" are displayed in galleries, exhibits, museums and private collections around the world. For most of his *Sunday in Hawai'i* shots, Brad turned to cooler venues away from the volcano, and captured the human eruptions of Big Islanders at play.

Ray Mains, an award-winning photographer from **Maui,** has gained a reputation for his aerial images of the Valley Isle and for a wide variety of scenic, commercial, portrait, and general Hawai'i stock images. His photos have appeared in *National Geographic, Time, Newsweek, Oceans, Skin Diver, USA*

Today, and other prominent publications, and such acclaimed books as *Maui On My Mind, Discovery: the Hawaiian Odyssey, The Hawaiian Canoe, Road to Hana,* and *Maui Bound.* Ray has produced over 100 postcards of Hawai'i, as well as posters of Makena Beach and Molokini. Ray spends his free time paddling with an outrigger canoe team, and as a sailor and scuba diver and NAUI diving instructor.

A recent transplant from Chicago, **Chris Mitts** lives in Honolulu on **O'ahu.** Her passions are hiking and photography, which she combines along some of the Island's wildest trails. A specialist in macro photography and portraiture, Chris begins her publishing bibliography with *Sunday In Hawai'i.*

Twain Newhart was born and raised on **O'ahu** and currently lives in Waikiki. Although his fashion photos have appeared in numerous Island publications, *Sunday In Hawai'i* presents his work for the first time in book form.

Lauren Lavonne Pritchett began her professional career in 1986 when she became the only triple winner in one of *Honolulu* magazine's annual photo contests. Since then she has traveled internationally each year, photographing the world's diverse landscapes and cultures, and publishing her work throughout Europe, South America, Australia, and Japan. Her most recent U.S. publications include *National Geographic World, Outside, Airline Pilot, Aviation, Surfing, Surfer,* and *Volleyball Magazine.* Lauren is currently expanding her artistic palette into the field of digital imaging with hi-tech computer graphics. She lives in Manoa Valley on **O'ahu.**

Born in Queens, New York, **Sri Maiava Rusden** was raised in Honolulu on **O'ahu,** and says, "I am Samoan Polish and the daughter of wrestler Neff Maiava." Sri has established herself as a fashion and lifestyle

photographer, with publication in *Honolulu, Guest Informant, Horizon Hawai'i,* and through Network Media, and Hagadone Publishing.

After spending many years in Hilo and Volcano on the Big Island, **Franco Salmoiraghi** moved back to Manoa Valley on **O'ahu** in 1983. Published internationally in magazines, his work also appears in many books including *Portfolio Hawai'i—The Big Island: Land of Fire & Ice; Christmas Island; In the Lee of Hualalai; Kaho'olawe: Na Leo o Kanaloa;* Roy Yamaguchi's *Feasts from Hawai'i;* Nana Veary's *Change We Must: My Spiritual Journey;* and *A Day in the Life of Hawaii.* Francos documentary images of the closing of Kau Sugar, Kaho'olawe, Waipi'o Valley, and the stone and concrete architectural ruins in Hawai'i have been exhibited and published extensively.

Gregg Alan Sonmore has established credentials in writing and photography, with publication in *New Times* magazine, and the newspapers *The Arizona Republic* and *Scottsdale Daily Press,* as well as commercial work for the Marriott Corporation and Stagebrush Theaters of Arizona. He has lived in Manoa Valley on **O'ahu** for ten years, and exhibits his specialty black-and-white "light-painting" urbanscapes in art galleries around Honolulu.

Julie Sotomura, raised in Honolulu on **O'ahu,** left to live and work on the mainland for ten years, then returned for ten years to live first on the North Shore and then in Honolulu, and is now relocated to San Francisco. For a while she was the news photographer for a daily in Colorado, and later expanded to commercial and editorial work, publishing in *Pacifica* and *Honolulu* magazines. This is Julie's first work in book format.

Michael T. Stewart lives in the rain forest of Hualalai, 1,000 feet above Kailua-Kona on the **Big Island.** His photography has garnered awards from National

Geographic Traveler Publications, Kodak, and the National Wildlife Federation, and has appeared in *Adventure West, Aloha, Spirit of Aloha, Hawai'i* magazine, and in books for the Hilton, Hyatt, Sheraton, Aston, and Outrigger hotels.

Underwater/Travel photojournalists **Cat & Kevin Sweeney** have lived on the volcanic flank of the **Big Island** for over 20 years. They have worked on assignment for the National Geographic Society, *Sports Illustrated,* Tourist Boards, and International Hotel Campaigns. Their images have been published in over fifteen countries on both sides of the equator, appeared nationally in *Newsweek, National Wildlife, Conde Nast Traveler, Sunset,* the *L.A. Times,* and illustrated numerous books, CD's, calendars, and editorials.

Brett Uprichard has been an editor and staff photographer at Honolulu Publishing Company since 1979. His photography has appeared in dozens of books and magazines, including *Honolulu, Spirit of Aloha, Island Business, Winds, Newsweek, Adweek, GEO, Reflections of Kauai, Under a Maui Sun, Kanyaku Imin, Waikiki Beachboys,* and *Hawaii Aloha.* He grew up in Kailua, **O'ahu,** in the 1950s, a place and time when every day seemed like Sunday.

The images of **Susan Aimee Weinik** have appeared through her work as a contributing photographer to *People Weekly,* and on assignment for *Time, Life, Sports Illustrated, Paris Match, The New York Times, Revlon,* and more. Susan is the owner/creator of *Hula-Grams,* a die-cut greeting card and publishing company. Her work has garnered several prestigious awards, including (by unanimous decision for the first time in the history of the Newswomen's Club of New York) the 1984 Front Page Award, and the 1986 Daily News Page One Award for Sports Feature Photography that appeared in *Sports Illustrated.* She lives in Kapahulu, on **O'ahu.**